*Shirlee Finley*

# PLANT BASED DIET COOKBOOK

# RECIPES FOR JUICES&SMOOTHIES

*More than 50 delicious, healthy and easy recipes for your Juices and Smoothies that will help you stay fit and detox your body*

© **Copyright 2021 - All rights reserved**.

This document is geared towards providing exact and reliable information in regard to the topic and issue covered.

- From a Declaration of Principles which was accepted and approved equally by a Committee of the American Bar Association and a Committee of Publishers and Associations.

In no way is it legal to reproduce, duplicate, or transmit any part of this document in either electronic means or in printed format. All rights reserved.

The information provided herein is stated to be truthful and consistent, in that any liability, in terms of inattention or otherwise, by any usage or abuse of any policies, processes, or directions contained within is the solitary and utter responsibility of the recipient reader. Under no circumstances will any legal responsibility or blame be held against the publisher for any reparation, damages, or monetary loss due to the information herein, either directly or indirectly.

Respective authors own all copyrights not held by the publisher.

The information herein is offered for informational purposes solely and is universal as so. The presentation of the information is without contract or any type of guarantee assurance.

The trademarks that are used are without any consent, and the publication of the trademark is without permission or backing by the trademark owner. All trademarks and brands within this book are for clarifying purposes only and are owned by the owners themselves, not affiliated with this document.

## Table of Contents

INTRODUCTION .................................................................................. 1

1. CLASSIC SWITCHEL ........................................................... 4
2. SMOOTHIE "APPLE PIE" ..................................................... 6
3. BEET AND CLEMENTINE PROTEIN SMOOTHIE ...................... 8
4. RED FRUIT SMMOTHIE ..................................................... 10
5. SUMMER SMOOTHIE ....................................................... 12
6. CHARD, LETTUCE, AND GINGER SMOOTHIE ....................... 14
7. BLUEBERRY AND BANANA SMOOTHIE ............................... 16
8. RED BEET, PEAR, AND APPLE SMOOTHIE .......................... 18
9. MATCHA LIMEADE ........................................................... 20
10. BANANA MILK ................................................................. 22
11. HAZELNUT AND CHOCOLATE MILK ................................... 24
12. APPLE, CARROT, CELERY, AND KALE JUICE ....................... 26
13. FRUIT INFUSED WATER ................................................... 28
14. SWEET AND SOUR JUICE ................................................. 30

| | | |
|---|---|---|
| 15. | Green Lemonade | 32 |
| 16. | Pineapple and Spinach Juice | 34 |
| 17. | Strawberry, Blueberry, and Banana Smoothie | 36 |
| 18. | Mango, Pineapple, and Banana Smoothie | 38 |
| 19. | Strawberry and Chocolate Milkshake | 40 |
| 20. | Berry and Yogurt Smoothie | 42 |
| 21. | Chocolate and Cherry Smoothie | 44 |
| 22. | Basil Lime Green Tea | 46 |
| 23. | Berry Lemonade Tea | 48 |
| 24. | Zobo Drink | 50 |
| 25. | Mango Agua Fresca | 52 |
| 26. | Light Ginger Tea | 54 |
| 27. | Swedish Glögg | 56 |
| 28. | Turmeric Coconut Milk | 58 |
| 29. | Kale Smoothie | 60 |
| 30. | Berry Smoothie | 62 |

| | | |
|---|---|---|
| 31. | CRANBERRY AND BANANA SMOOTHIE | 64 |
| 32. | HOT TROPICAL SMOOTHIE | 66 |
| 33. | PUMPKIN SMOOTHIE | 68 |
| 34. | KIWI AND STRAWBERRY SMOOTHIE | 70 |
| 35. | SUPER SMOOTHIE | 72 |
| 36. | MINT CHOCOLATE GREEN PROTEIN SMOOTHIE | 74 |
| 37. | VEGAN GREEN AVOCADO SMOOTHIE | 76 |
| 38. | THE HUSBAND PROTEIN SMOOTHIE | 78 |
| 39. | BLUEBERRY SMOOTHIE BOWL | 80 |
| 40. | MAX POWER SMOOTHIE | 82 |
| 41. | PINK PANTHER SMOOTHIE | 84 |
| 42. | CHOCOLATE PB SMOOTHIE | 86 |
| 43. | SIMPLE DATE SHAKE | 88 |
| 44. | BANANA NUT SMOOTHIE | 90 |
| 45. | CHAI CHIA SMOOTHIE | 92 |
| 46. | HYDRATION STATION | 94 |

| | | |
|---|---|---|
| 47. | Mango Madness | 96 |
| 48. | "Frosty" Chocolate Shake | 98 |
| 49. | Chocolate Peanut Butter Shake | 100 |
| 50. | Chia Coffee Mix | 102 |
| 51. | Lime and Cucumber Electrolyte Drink | 104 |
| 52. | Plant-Based Strawberry Cream | 106 |
| 53. | Tropi-Kale Breeze | 108 |
| CONCLUSION | | 110 |

# Introduction

Modern life is hectic and so are we as a result: we don't have time to do anything, not even to linger in the kitchen to prepare a complete and balanced meal. For this reason, smoothies and juices are an excellent alternative: rich in vitamins and antioxidants, low-calorie, simple and quick to prepare, you just need a good blender and seasonal fruit to enjoy a tasty snack, a post-workout drink or a breakfast that replaces packaged products.

If you add some green leafy vegetables to the fruit, you will obtain a natural drink rich in therapeutic virtues. Just think that smoothies of this type are indicated to treat diseases such as depression, memory loss, high cholesterol, obesity, cardiovascular disease and more.

If you don't want to limit yourself to a simple mix of ingredients blended, you can try the real "smoothies", a term that is slowly entering our lexicon as well, since many vegetarian or vegan places have started to propose them massively. But what is a smoothie? It is essentially a mix of ingredients blended together made up of three elements: the liquid part which can be water, fruit juice, tea; the basic ingredients such as fruits, vegetables, nuts and seeds; the "cold" element given by frozen fruits or vegetables, ice and cold liquids.

You can make smoothies with an exceptional taste, the only limit in these cases is your imagination, moreover the great advantage of the smoothie is that you can always "correct" it according to your taste by simply tasting it often and adding fruit, juices or citrus peels to achieve a balanced flavor.

Below you will find the ingredients for some common smoothies and other more unusual ones, feel free to try according to your taste and your ideas, mix colors, different textures, nutritional values, make the most of what nature offers us!

# JUICES & SMOOTHIES

# 1. Classic Switchel

**Preparation time:** 5 minutes.

**Cooking time:** 0 minutes.

**Servings:** 4

**Ingredients:**
- 1-inch piece ginger, minced
- 2 tablespoons apple cider vinegar
- 2 tablespoons maple syrup
- 4 cups water
- ¼ teaspoon sea salt, optional

**Directions:**
1. Combine all the ingredients in a glass. Stir to mix well.
2. Serve immediately or chill in the refrigerator for an hour before serving.

**Nutrition:**
- **Calories:** 110
- **Fat:** 0g
- **Carbs:** 28.0g
- **Fiber:** 0g
- **Protein:** 0g

## 2. Smoothie "Apple Pie"

**Preparation time:** 5 minutes.

**Cooking time:** 0 minutes.

**Servings:** 2

**Ingredients:**
- 1 cup of unsweetened almond milk
- 1 cup of mashed apple
- 1/2 cup of raw, unsalted cashews soaked overnight
- 2 tablespoons of maple syrup (or 2 dates soaked overnight)
- 2 tablespoons of vanilla extract
- ½ teaspoon of cinnamon powder
- 1 cup of ice

**Directions:**
1. Combine all the ingredients in a food processor, then pulse on high for 1 minute or until glossy and creamy.
2. Enjoy your sip of apple pie!

**Nutrition:**
- **Calories:** 431
- **Fat:** 21.25g
- **Carbs:** 47.17g
- **Sodium:** 9.35g
- **Protein:** 10.1g
- **Potassium:** 5,10g
- **Calcium:** 1,80g

## 3. Beet and Clementine Protein Smoothie

**Preparation time:** 10 minutes.

**Cooking time:** 0 minutes.

**Servings:** 3

**Ingredients:**
- 1 small beet, peeled and chopped
- 1 clementine, peeled and broken into segments
- ½ ripe banana
- ½ cup raspberries
- 1 tablespoon chia seeds
- 2 tablespoons almond butter
- ¼ teaspoon vanilla extract
- 1 cup unsweetened almond milk
- 1/8 teaspoon fine sea salt, optional

**Directions:**
3. Combine all the ingredients in a food processor, then pulse on high for 2 minutes or until glossy and creamy.
4. Refrigerate for an hour and serve chilled.

**Nutrition:**
- **Calories:** 526
- **Fat:** 25.4g
- **Carbs:** 61.9g
- **Fiber:** 17.3g
- **Protein:** 20.6g

## 4. Red Fruit Smmothie

**Preparation time:** 10 minutes.

**Cooking time:** 0 minutes.

**Servings:** 2

**Ingredients:**
- 2 pots of soy yogurt
- 1 cup of strawberries
- 1 cup of raspberries
- 1 cup of red fruits
- 3 or 4 tablespoons of almond milk
- 1 tablespoon of honey

**Directions:**
1. Combine all the ingredients in a food processor, then pulse on high for 2 minutes or until glossy and creamy.
2. Refrigerate for an hour and serve chilled.

**Nutrition (for 100ml):**
- **Calories:** 46
- **Fat:** 1.30g
- **Carbs:** 6.90g
- **Fiber:** 2.3g
- **Protein:** 2.g

## 5. Summer Smoothie

**Preparation time:** 5 minutes

**Cooking time:** 0 minutes.

**Servings:** 2

**Ingredients:**
- 2 cups of di fresh spinach
- 1 cup of diced pineapple
- 2 bananas
- 1 cup of diced mango
- 2 cups of water

**Directions:**
1. Place the spinach together with the water in a food processor and blend well.
2. Add all the other ingredients and pulse for 2 to 3 minutes at high speed until smooth.
3. Pour the smoothie into two glasses and then serve.

**Nutrition (1 portion):**
- **Calories:** 285
- **Fat:** 1.4g
- **Carbs:** 72.70g
- **Protein:** 3.9g
- **Fiber:** 6.6g

## 6. Chard, Lettuce, and Ginger Smoothie

**Preparation time:** 5 minutes

**Cooking time:** 0 minutes.

**Servings:** 2

**Ingredients:**
- 10 chard leaves, chopped
- 1-inch piece of ginger, chopped
- 10 lettuce leaves, chopped
- ½ teaspoon black salt
- 2 pears, chopped
- 2 teaspoons coconut sugar
- ¼ teaspoon ground black pepper
- ¼ teaspoon salt
- 2 tablespoons lemon juice
- 2 cups of water

**Directions:**
1. Place all the ingredients in the order in a food processor or blender and then pulse for 2 to 3 minutes at high speed until smooth.
2. Pour the smoothie into two glasses and then serve.

**Nutrition:**
- **Calories:** 514
- **Fat:** 0g
- **Carbs:** 15g
- **Protein:** 4g
- **Fiber:** 4g

# 7. Blueberry and Banana Smoothie

**Preparation time:** 5 minutes.

**Cooking time:** 0 minutes.

**Servings:** 2

**Ingredients:**
- 2 frozen bananas
- 2 cups frozen blueberries
- 2 cups almond milk, unsweetened
- 1/2 teaspoon or so cinnamon
- A dash of vanilla extract

**Directions:**
1. Place all the ingredients in the order in a food processor or blender and then pulse for 2 to 3 minutes at high speed until smooth.
2. Pour the smoothie into two glasses and then serve.

**Nutrition:**
- **Calories:** 244
- **Fat:** 3.8g
- **Carbs:** 51.5g
- **Protein:** 4g
- **Fiber:** 7.3g

## 8. Red Beet, Pear, and Apple Smoothie

**Preparation time:** 5 minutes.

**Cooking time:** 0 minutes.

**Servings:** 2

**Ingredients:**
- 1/2 of medium beet, peeled, chopped
- 1 tablespoon chopped cilantro
- 1 orange, juiced
- 1 medium pear, chopped
- 1 mcdium apple, cored, chopped
- 1/4 teaspoon ground black pepper
- 1/8 teaspoon rock salt
- 1 teaspoon coconut sugar
- 1/4 teaspoons salt
- 1 cup of water

**Directions:**
1. Place all the ingredients in the order in a food processor or blender and then pulse for 2 to 3 minutes at high speed until smooth.
2. Pour the smoothie into two glasses and then serve.

**Nutrition:**
- **Calories:** 132
- **Fat:** 0g
- **Carbs:** 34g
- **Protein:** 1g
- **Fiber:** 5g

## 9. Matcha Limeade

**Preparation time:** 10 minutes.

**Cooking time:** 0 minutes.

**Servings:** 4

**Ingredients:**
- 2 tablespoons matcha powder
- ¼ cup raw agave syrup
- 3 cups water, divided
- 1 cup fresh lime juice
- 3 tablespoons chia seeds

**Directions:**
1. Lightly simmer the matcha, agave syrup, and 1 cup of water in a saucepan over medium heat. Keep stirring until no matcha lumps.
2. Pour the matcha mixture into a large glass, add the remaining ingredients, and mix well.
3. Refrigerate for at least an hour before serving.

**Nutrition:**
- **Calories:** 152
- **Fat:** 4.5g
- **Carbs:** 26.8g
- **Fiber:** 5.3g
- **Protein:** 3.7g

## 10. Banana Milk

**Preparation time:** 5 minutes.

**Cooking time:** 0 minutes.

**Servings:** 2

**Ingredients:**
- 2 dates
- 2 medium bananas, peeled
- 1 teaspoon vanilla extract, unsweetened
- 1/2 cup ice
- 2 cups of water

**Directions:**
1. Place all the ingredients in the order in a food processor or blender and then pulse for 2 to 3 minutes at high speed until smooth.
2. Pour the smoothie into two glasses and then serve.

**Nutrition:**
- **Calories:** 79
- **Fat:** 0g
- **Carbs:** 19.8g
- **Protein:** 0.8g
- **Fiber:** 6g

## 11. Hazelnut and Chocolate Milk

**Preparation time:** 5 minutes.

**Cooking time:** 0 minutes.

**Servings:** 2

**Ingredients:**
- 2 tablespoons cocoa powder
- 4 dates, pitted
- 1 cup hazelnuts
- 3 cups of water

**Direction:**
1. Place all the ingredients in the order in a food processor or blender and then pulse for 2 to 3 minutes at high speed until smooth.
2. Pour the smoothie into two glasses and then serve.

**Nutrition:**
- **Calories:** 120
- **Fat:** 5g
- **Carbs:** 19g
- **Protein:** 2g
- **Fiber:** 1g

# 12. Apple, Carrot, Celery, and Kale Juice

**Preparation time:** 5 minutes.

**Cooking time:** 0 minutes.

**Servings**: 2

**Ingredients:**
- 5 curly kale
- 2 green apples, cored, peeled, chopped
- 2 large stalks celery
- 4 large carrots, cored, peeled, chopped

**Directions:**
1. Process all the ingredients in the order in a juicer or blender and then strain it into two glasses.
2. Serve straight away.

**Nutrition:**
- **Calories:** 183
- **Fat:** 2.5g
- **Carbs:** 46g
- **Protein:** 13g
- **Fiber:** 3g

## 13. Fruit Infused Water

**Preparation time:** 5 minutes.

**Cooking time:** 0 minutes.

**Servings:** 2

**Ingredients:**
- 3 strawberries, sliced
- 5 mint leaves
- ½ of orange, sliced
- 2 cups of water

**Directions:**
1. Divide fruits and mint between two glasses, pour in water, stir until just mixed, and refrigerate for 2 hours.
2. Serve straight away.

**Nutrition:**
- **Calories:** 5.4
- **Fat:** 0.1g
- **Carbs:** 1.3g
- **Protein:** 0.1g
- **Fiber:** 0.4g

## 14. Sweet and Sour Juice

**Preparation time:** 5 minutes.

**Cooking time:** 0 minutes.

**Servings:** 2

**Ingredients:**
- 2 medium apples, cored, peeled, chopped
- 2 large cucumbers, peeled
- 4 cups chopped grapefruit
- 1 cup mint

**Directions:**
1. Process all the ingredients in the order in a juicer or blender and then strain it into two glasses.
2. Serve straight away.

**Nutrition:**
- **Calories:** 90
- **Fat:** 0g
- **Carbs:** 23g
- **Protein:** 0g
- **Fiber:** 9g

## 15. Green Lemonade

**Preparation time:** 5 minutes.

**Cooking time:** 0 minutes.

**Servings**: 2

**Ingredients:**
- 10 large stalks of celery, chopped
- 2 medium green apples, cored, peeled, chopped
- 2 medium cucumbers, peeled, chopped
- 2 inches' piece of ginger
- 10 stalks of kale, chopped
- 2 cups parsley

**Directions:**
1. Process all the ingredients in the order in a juicer or blender and then strain it into two glasses.
2. Serve straight away.

**Nutrition:**
- **Calories:** 102.3
- **Fat:** 1.1g
- **Carbs:** 26.2g
- **Protein:** 4.7g
- **Fiber:** 8.5g

# 16. Pineapple and Spinach Juice

**Preparation time:** 5 minutes.

**Cooking time:** 0 minutes.

**Servings:** 2

**Ingredients:**
- 2 medium red apples, cored, peeled, chopped
- 3 cups spinach
- ½ of a medium pineapple, peeled
- 2 lemons, peeled

**Directions:**
1. Process all the ingredients in the order in a juicer or blender and then strain it into two glasses.
2. Serve straight away.

**Nutrition:**
- **Calories:** 131
- **Fat:** 0.5g
- **Carbs:** 34.5g
- **Protein:** 1.7g
- **Fiber:** 5g

## 17. Strawberry, Blueberry, and Banana Smoothie

**Preparation time:** 5 minutes.

**Cooking time:** 0 minutes.

**Servings:** 2

**Ingredients:**
- 1 tablespoon hulled hemp seeds
- ½ cup of frozen strawberries
- 1 small frozen banana
- ½ cup frozen blueberries
- 2 tablespoons cashew butter
- ¾ cup cashew milk, unsweetened

**Directions:**
1. Place all the ingredients in the order in a food processor or blender and then pulse for 2 to 3 minutes at high speed until smooth.
2. Pour the smoothie into two glasses and then serve.

**Nutrition:**
- **Calories:** 334
- **Fat:** 17g
- **Carbs:** 46g
- **Protein:** 7g
- **Fiber:** 7g

## 18. Mango, Pineapple, and Banana Smoothie

**Preparation time:** 5 minutes.

**Cooking time:** 0 minutes.

**Servings**: 2

**Ingredients:**
- 2 cups pineapple chunks
- 2 frozen bananas
- 2 medium mangoes, pitted, cut into chunks
- 1 cup almond milk, unsweetened
- Chia seeds as needed for garnishing

**Directions:**
1. Place all the ingredients in the order in a food processor or blender and then pulse for 2 to 3 minutes at high speed until smooth.
2. Pour the smoothie into two glasses and then serve.

**Nutrition:**
- **Calories:** 287
- **Fat:** 1.2g
- **Carbs:** 73.3g
- **Protein:** 3.5g
- **Fiber:** 8g

# 19. Strawberry and Chocolate Milkshake

**Preparation time:** 5 minutes.

**Cooking time:** 0 minutes.

**Servings:** 2

**Ingredients:**
- 2 cups frozen strawberries
- 3 tablespoons cocoa powder
- 1 scoop protein powder
- 2 tablespoons maple syrup
- 1 teaspoon vanilla extract, unsweetened
- 2 cups almond milk, unsweetened

**Directions:**
1. Place all the ingredients in the order in a food processor or blender and then pulse for 2 to 3 minutes at high speed until smooth.
2. Pour the smoothie into two glasses and then serve.

**Nutrition:**
- **Calories:** 199
- **Fat:** 4.1g
- **Carbs:** 40.5g
- **Protein:** 3.7g
- **Fiber:** 5.5g

## 20. Berry and Yogurt Smoothie

**Preparation time:** 5 minutes.

**Cooking time:** 0 minutes.

**Servings**: 2

**Ingredients:**
- 2 small bananas
- 3 cups frozen mixed berries
- 1(½) cup cashew yogurt
- 1/2 teaspoon vanilla extract, unsweetened
- 1/2 cup almond milk, unsweetened

**Directions:**
1. Place all the ingredients in the order in a food processor or blender and then pulse for 2 to 3 minutes at high speed until smooth.
2. Pour the smoothie into two glasses and then serve.

**Nutrition:**
- **Calories:** 326
- **Fat:** 6.5g
- **Carbs:** 65.6g
- **Protein:** 8g
- **Fiber:** 8.4g

# 21. Chocolate and Cherry Smoothie

**Preparation time:** 5 minutes.

**Cooking time:** 0 minutes.

**Servings:** 2

**Ingredients:**
- 4 cups frozen cherries
- 2 tablespoons cocoa powder
- 1 scoop of protein powder
- 1 teaspoon maple syrup
- 2 cups almond milk, unsweetened

**Directions:**
1. Place all the ingredients in the order in a food processor or blender and then pulse for 2 to 3 minutes at high speed until smooth.
2. Pour the smoothie into two glasses and then serve.

**Nutrition:**
- **Calories:** 324
- **Fat:** 5g
- **Carbs:** 75.1g
- **Protein:** 7.2g
- **Fiber:** 11.3g

## 22. Basil Lime Green Tea

**Preparation time:** 5 minutes.

**Cooking time:** 4 minutes.

**Servings:** 8

**Ingredients:**
- 8 cups of filtered water
- 10 bags of green tea
- ¼ cup of honey
- A pinch of baking soda
- Lime slices to taste
- Lemon slices to taste
- Basil leaves to taste

**Directions:**
1. Add water, honey, and baking soda to the pot and mix. Add the tea bags and cover. Cook overhigh heat for 4 minutes. Open and serve with lime slices, lemon slices, and basil leaves.

**Nutrition:**
- **Calories:**32
- **Carbs:**8g
- **Fat:**0g
- **Protein:**0g

## 23. Berry Lemonade Tea

**Preparation time:** 5 minutes.

**Cooking time:** 12 minutes.

**Servings:** 4

**Ingredients:**
- 3 tea bags
- 2 cups of natural lemonade
- 1 cup of frozen mixed berries
- 2 cups of water
- 1 lemon, sliced

**Directions:**
1. Put everything in the Instant Pot and cover. Cook over high heat for 12 minutes. Open, strain, and serve.

**Nutrition:**
- **Calories:** 21
- **Carbs:** 8g
- **Fat:** 0.2g
- **Protein:** 0.4g

## 24. Zobo Drink

**Preparation time:** 5 minutes.

**Cooking time:** 10 minutes.

**Servings:** 8

**Ingredients:**
- 2 cups dried hibiscus petals (zobo leaves), rinsed
- Pineapple rind from 1 pineapple
- 1 cup of granulated sugar
- 1 teaspoon fresh ginger, grated
- 10 cups of water

**Directions:**
1. Add water, ginger, and sugar into the pot and mix well.
2. Then add zobo leaves and pineapple rind.
3. Cover and cook overhigh heat for 10 minutes. Open and discard solids.
4. Chill and serve.

**Nutrition:**
- **Calories:** 65
- **Carbs:** 7g
- **Fat:** 2.6g
- **Protein:** 1.14g

## 25. Mango Agua Fresca

**Preparation time:** 5 minutes.

**Cooking time:** 0 minutes.

**Servings:** 2

**Ingredients:**
- 2 fresh mangoes, diced
- 1(½) cups water
- 1 teaspoon fresh lime juice
- Maple syrup to taste
- 2 cups ice
- 2 slices fresh lime, for garnish
- 2 fresh mint sprigs, for garnish

**Directions:**
1. Put the mangoes, lime juice, maple syrup, and water in a blender. Process until creamy and smooth.
2. Divide the beverage into two glasses, then garnish each glass with ice, lime slice, and mint sprig before serving.

**Nutrition:**
- **Calories:** 230
- **Fat:** 1.3g
- **Carbs:** 57.7g
- **Fiber:** 5.4g
- **Protein:** 2.8g

## 26. Light Ginger Tea

**Preparation time:** 5 minutes.

**Cooking time:** 10 to 15 minutes.

**Servings:** 2

**Ingredients:**
- 1 small ginger knob, sliced into four 1-inch chunks
- 4 cups water
- Juice of 1 large lemon
- Maple syrup to taste

**Directions:**
1. Add the ginger knob and water in a saucepan, then simmer over medium heat for 10 to 15 minutes.
2. Turn off the heat, then mix in the lemon juice. Strain the liquid to remove the ginger, then fold in the maple syrup and serve.

**Nutrition:**
- **Calories:** 32
- **Fat:** 0.1g
- **Carbs:** 8.6g
- **Fiber:** 0.1g
- **Protein:** 0.1g

## 27. Swedish Glögg

**Preparation time:** 5 minutes.

**Cooking time:** 15 minutes.

**Servings:** 1

**Ingredients:**
- ½ cup of orange juice
- ½ cup of water
- 1 piece of ginger cut into ½ pieces
- 1 whole clove
- 1 opened cardamom pods
- 2 tablespoons orange zest
- 1 cinnamon stick
- 1 whole allspice
- 1 vanilla bean

**Directions:**
1. Add everything in the pot. Cover and cook overhigh heat for 15 minutes. Open and serve.

**Nutrition:**
- **Calories** 194
- **Carbs** 41g
- **Fat** 3g
- **Protein** 1.7g

## 28. Turmeric Coconut Milk

**Preparation time:** 5 minutes.

**Cooking time:** 15 minutes.

**Servings:** 8

**Ingredients:**
- 13.5 ounces coconut milk
- 3 cups of filtered water
- 2 teaspoons turmeric powder
- 3 whole cloves
- 2 cinnamon sticks
- ½ teaspoon ginger powder
- A pinch of pepper
- 2 tablespoons honey

**Directions:**
1. Place everything except the honey in the pot. Cover and cook overhigh heat for 15 minutes. Remove cloves and cinnamon sticks. Add honey, mix and serve.

**Nutrition:**
- **Calories:** 42
- **Carbs:** 9g
- **Fat:** 0g
- **Protein:** 0g

## 29. Kale Smoothie

**Preparation time:** 5 minutes.

**Cooking time:** 0 minutes.

**Servings:** 2

**Ingredients:**
- 2 cups chopped kale leaves
- 1 banana, peeled
- 1 cup frozen strawberries
- 1 cup unsweetened almond milk
- 4 Medjool dates, pitted and chopped

**Directions:**
1. Put all the ingredients in a food processor, then process until glossy and smooth.
2. Serve immediately or chill in the refrigerator for an hour before serving.

**Nutrition:**
- **Calories:** 663
- **Fat:** 10.0g
- **Carbs:** 142.5g
- **Fiber:** 19.0g
- **Protein:** 17.4g

## 30. Berry Smoothie

**Preparation time:** 5 minutes.

**Cooking time:** 0 minutes.

**Servings:** 4

**Ingredients:**
- 1 cup berry mix (strawberries, blueberries, and cranberries)
- 4 Medjool dates, pitted and chopped
- 1(½) cups unsweetened almond milk, plus more as needed

**Directions:**
1. Add all the ingredients to a blender, then process until the mixture is smooth and well mixed.
2. Serve immediately or chill in the refrigerator for an hour before serving.

**Nutrition:**
- **Calories:** 473
- **Fat:** 4.0g
- **Carbs:** 103.7g
- **Fiber:** 9.7g
- **Protein:** 14.8g

# 31. Cranberry and Banana Smoothie

**Preparation time:** 5 minutes.

**Cooking time:** 0 minutes.

**Servings:** 4

**Ingredients:**
- 1 cup frozen cranberries
- 1 large banana, peeled
- 4 Medjool dates, pitted and chopped
- 1(½) cups unsweetened almond milk

**Directions:**
1. Add all the ingredients to a food processor, then process until the mixture is glossy and well mixed.
2. Serve immediately or chill in the refrigerator for an hour before serving.

**Nutrition:**
- **Calories:** 616
- **Fat:** 8.0g
- **Carbs:** 132.8g
- **Fiber:** 14.6g
- **Protein:** 15.7g

## 32. Hot Tropical Smoothie

**Preparation time:** 5 minutes.

**Cooking time:** 0 minutes.

**Servings:** 4

**Ingredients:**
- 1 cup frozen mango chunks
- 1 cup frozen pineapple chunks
- 1 small tangerine, peeled and pitted
- 2 cups spinach leaves
- 1 cup coconut water
- ¼ teaspoon cayenne pepper, optional

**Directions:**
1. Add all the ingredients to a food processor, then process until the mixture is smooth and combine well.
2. Serve immediately or chill in the refrigerator for an hour before serving.

**Nutrition:**
- **Calories:** 283
- **Fat:** 1.9g
- **Carbs:** 67.9g
- **Fiber:** 10.4g
- **Protein:** 6.4g

## 33. Pumpkin Smoothie

**Preparation time:** 5 minutes.

**Cooking time:** 0 minutes.

**Servings:** 5

**Ingredients:**
- ½ cup pumpkin purée
- 4 Medjool dates, pitted and chopped
- 1 cup unsweetened almond milk
- ¼ teaspoon vanilla extract
- ¼ teaspoon ground cinnamon
- ½ cup ice
- Pinch ground nutmeg

**Directions:**
1. Add all the ingredients in a blender, then process until the mixture is glossy and well mixed.
2. Serve immediately.

**Nutrition:**
- **Calories:** 417
- **Fat:** 3.0g
- **Carbs:** 94.9g
- **Fiber:** 10.4g
- **Protein:** 11.4g

## 34. Kiwi and Strawberry Smoothie

**Preparation time:** 5 minutes.

**Cooking time:** 0 minutes.

**Servings:** 3

**Ingredients:**
- 1 kiwi, peeled
- 5 medium strawberries
- ½ frozen banana
- 1 cup unsweetened almond milk
- 2 tablespoons hemp seeds
- 2 tablespoons peanut butter
- 1 to 2 teaspoons maple syrup
- ½ cup spinach leaves
- Handful broccoli sprouts

**Directions:**
1. Put all the ingredients in a food processor, then process until creamy and smooth.
2. Serve immediately or chill in the refrigerator for an hour before serving.

**Nutrition:**
- **Calories:** 562
- **Fat:** 28.6g
- **Carbs:** 63.6g
- **Fiber:** 15.1g
- **Protein:** 23.3g

## 35. Super Smoothie

**Preparation time:** 5 minutes.

**Cooking time:** 0 minutes.

**Servings:** 4

**Ingredients:**
- 1 banana, peeled
- 1 cup chopped mango
- 1 cup raspberries
- ¼ cup rolled oats
- 1 carrot, peeled
- 1 cup chopped fresh kale
- 2 tablespoons chopped fresh parsley
- 1 tablespoon flaxseeds
- 1 tablespoon grated fresh ginger
- ½ cup unsweetened soy milk
- 1 cup water

**Directions:**
1. Put all the ingredients in a food processor, then process until glossy and smooth.
2. Serve immediately or chill in the refrigerator for an hour before serving.

**Nutrition:**
- **Calories:** 550
- **Fat:** 39.0g
- **Carbs:** 31.0g
- **Fiber:** 15.0g
- **Protein:** 13.0g

## 36. Mint Chocolate Green Protein Smoothie

**Preparation time:** 5 minutes.

**Cooking time:** 0 minutes.

**Servings:** 1

**Ingredients:**
- 1 scoop chocolate powder
- 1 tablespoon flaxseed
- 1 banana
- 1 mint leaf
- 3/4 cup almond milk
- 3 tablespoons dark chocolate (chopped)

**Directions:**
1. Blend all the ingredients, except the dark chocolate. Garnish dark chocolate when ready.

**Nutrition:**
- **Calories:** 115
- **Carbs:** 22g
- **Fat:** 2g
- **Protein:** 6g

## 37. Vegan Green Avocado Smoothie

**Preparation time:** 5 minutes.

**Cooking time:** 0 minutes.

**Servings:** 2

**Ingredients:**
- 1 banana
- 1 cup of water
- 1/2 avocado
- 1/2 lemon juice
- 1/2 cup coconut yogurt

**Directions:**
1. Blend all the ingredients until smooth. Serve.

**Nutrition:**
- **Calories:** 299
- **Fat:** 1.1g
- **Carbohydrates:** 1.5g
- **Protein:** 7.9g

## 38. The Husband Protein Smoothie

**Preparation time:** 3 minutes.

**Cooking time:** 0 minutes.

**Servings:** 1

**Ingredients:**
- 1/4 cup rolled oats
- 1 cup wild blueberries, frozen
- 1-inch fresh ginger, peeled and diced
- 1 cup strawberries, frozen
- 3 tablespoons hulled hemp seeds
- 2 cups baby spinach
- 2 tablespoons almond butter
- 2 tablespoons maple syrup
- 1(1/4) cup of water

**Directions:**
1. Add all the ingredients into the blender and blend for a minute or until it looks smooth.

**Nutrition:**
- **Calories:** 680
- **Carbs:** 84g
- **Proteins:** 21g
- **Fat:** 36g

## 39. Blueberry Smoothie Bowl

**Preparation time:** 5 minutes.

**Cooking time:** 0 minutes.

**Servings:** 2

**Ingredients:**
- 1 tablespoon ground flaxseed
- 1 medium banana
- 4 ice cubes
- 1 cup blueberries
- ¾ cup unsweetened almond milk
- 1 tablespoon maple syrup
- ¼ cup nuts chopped

**Directions:**
1. Blend all the ingredients in a high-speed blender. Garnish with chopped nuts and mint leaves. Serve and enjoy!

**Nutrition:**
- **Calories:** 335
- **Carbs:** 61g
- **Fat:** 5g
- **Protein:** 10g

## 40. Max Power Smoothie

**Preparation time:** 5 minutes.

**Cooking time:** 0 minutes.

**Servings:** 3–4

**Ingredients:**
- 1 banana
- ¼ cup rolled oats or 1 scoop plant protein powder
- 1 tablespoon flaxseed or chia seeds
- 1 cup raspberries or other berries
- 1 cup chopped mango (frozen or fresh)
- ½ cup non-dairy milk (optional)
- 1 cup of water
- Bonus boosters (optional):
- 2 tablespoons fresh parsley, or basil, chopped
- 1 cup chopped fresh kale, spinach, collards, or other greens
- 1 carrot, peeled
- 1 tablespoon grated fresh ginger

**Directions:**
1. Purée everything in a blender until smooth, adding more water (or non-dairy milk) if needed. Add none, some, or all the bonus boosters, as desired. Purée until blended.

**Nutrition:**
- **Calories:** 550
- **Fat:** 9g
- **Carbs:** 116g
- **Protein:** 13g

# 41. Pink Panther Smoothie

**Preparation time:** 5 minutes.

**Cooking time:** 0 minutes.

**Servings:** 3

**Ingredients:**
- 1 cup strawberries
- 1 cup chopped melon (any kind)
- 1 cup cranberries or raspberries
- 1 tablespoon chia seeds
- ½ cup coconut milk, or other non-dairy milk
- 1 cup of water

**Bonus boosters (optional):**
- 1 teaspoon Goji berries
- 2 tablespoons fresh mint, chopped

**Directions:**
1. Purée everything in a blender until smooth, adding more water (or coconut milk) if needed. Add bonus boosters, as desired. Purée until blended.

**Nutrition:**
- **Calories:** 459
- **Fat:** 30g
- **Carbs:** 52g
- **Protein:** 8g

## 42. Chocolate PB Smoothie

**Preparation time:** 5 minutes.

**Cooking time:** 0 minutes.

**Servings:** 3-4

**Ingredients:**
- 1 banana
- ¼ cup rolled oats or 1 scoop plant protein powder
- 1 tablespoon flaxseed or chia seeds
- 1 tablespoon unsweetened cocoa powder
- 1 tablespoon peanut butter, or almond or sunflower seed butter
- 1 tablespoon maple syrup (optional)
- 1 cup alfalfa sprouts or spinach, chopped (optional)
- ½ cup non-dairy milk (optional)
- 1 cup of water

**Bonus boosters (optional):**
- 1 teaspoon maca powder
- 1 teaspoon cocoa nibs

**Directions:**
1. Purée everything in a blender until smooth, adding more water (or non-dairy milk) if needed. Add bonus boosters, as desired. Purée until blended.

**Nutrition:**
- **Calories:** 474
- **Fat:** 16g
- **Carbs:** 79g
- **Protein:** 13g

## 43. Simple Date Shake

**Preparation time:** 10 minutes.

**Cooking time:** 0 minutes.

**Servings:** 2

**Ingredients:**
- 5 Medjool dates, pitted, soaked in boiling water for 5 minutes
- ¾ cup unsweetened coconut milk
- 1 teaspoon vanilla extract
- ½ teaspoon fresh lemon juice
- ¼ teaspoon sea salt, optional
- 1(½) cups ice

**Directions:**
1. Put all the ingredients in a food processor, then process until it has a milkshake and smooth texture.
2. Serve immediately.

**Nutrition:**
- **Calories:** 380
- **Fat:** 21.6g
- **Carbs:** 50.3g
- **Fiber:** 6.0g
- **Protein:** 3.2g

## 44. Banana Nut Smoothie

**Preparation time:** 5 minutes.

**Cooking time:** 0 minutes.

**Servings:** 2–3

**Ingredients:**
- 1 banana
- 1 tablespoon almond butter/sunflower seed butter
- ¼ teaspoon ground cinnamon
- Pinch ground nutmeg
- 1 to 2 tablespoons dates or maple syrup
- 1 tablespoon ground flaxseed, or chia, or hemp hearts
- ½ cup non-dairy milk (optional)
- 1 cup of water

**Directions:**
1. Purée everything in a blender until smooth, adding more water (or non-dairy milk) if needed.

**Nutrition:**
- **Calories:** 343
- **Fat:** 14g
- **Carbs:** 55g
- **Protein:** 6g

## 45.     Chai Chia Smoothie

**Preparation time:** 5 minutes.

**Cooking time:** 0 minutes.

**Servings:** 3

**Ingredients:**
- 1 banana
- ½ cup of coconut milk
- 1 cup of water
- 1 cup alfalfa sprouts (optional)
- 1 to 2 soft Medjool dates, pitted
- 1 tablespoon chia seeds/ground flax or hemp hearts
- ¼ teaspoon ground cinnamon
- Pinch ground cardamom
- 1 tablespoon grated fresh ginger or ¼ teaspoon ground ginger

**Directions:**
1. Purée everything in a blender until smooth, adding more water (or coconut milk) if needed.

**Nutrition:**
- **Calories:** 477
- **Fat:** 29g
- **Carbs:** 57g
- **Protein:** 8g

## 46. Hydration Station

**Preparation time:** 5 minutes.

**Cooking time:** 0 minutes.

**Servings:** 3–4

**Ingredients:**
- 1 banana
- 1 orange, peeled and sectioned, or 1 cup pure orange juice
- 1 cup strawberries (frozen or fresh)
- 1 cup chopped cucumber
- ½ cup of coconut water
- 1 cup of water
- ½ cup ice

**Bonus boosters (optional):**
- 1 cup chopped spinach
- ¼ cup fresh mint, chopped

**Directions:**
1. Purée everything in a blender until smooth, adding more water if needed. Add bonus boosters, as desired. Purée until blended.

**Nutrition:**
- **Calories:** 320
- **Fat:** 3g
- **Carbs:** 76g
- **Protein:** 6g

## 47. Mango Madness

**Preparation time:** 5 minutes.

**Cooking time:** 0 minutes.

**Servings:** 3–4

**Ingredients:**
- 1 banana
- 1 cup chopped mango (frozen or fresh)
- 1 cup chopped peach (frozen or fresh)
- 1 cup strawberries
- 1 carrot, peeled and chopped (optional)
- 1 cup of water

**Directions:**
1. Purée everything in a blender until smooth, adding more water if needed.

**Nutrition:**
- **Calories:** 376
- **Fat:** 2g
- **Carbs:** 95g
- **Protein:** 5g

## 48. "Frosty" Chocolate Shake

**Preparation time:** 40 minutes.

**Cooking time:** 0 minutes.

**Servings:** 2

**Ingredients:**
- 1 cup heavy (whipping) cream/coconut cream
- 2 tablespoons unsweetened cocoa powder
- 1 tablespoon almond butter
- 1 teaspoon vanilla extract
- 5 or 6 drops liquid stevia

**Directions:**
1. Beat the cream in a medium bowl or using a stand mixer until fluffy, 3 to 4 minutes. Add the cocoa powder, almond butter, vanilla, and stevia.
2. Beat the mixture for an additional 2 to 3 minutes, or until the mixture has the consistency of whipped cream. Place the bowl in the freezer for 25 to 30 minutes before serving.

**Nutrition:**
- **Calories:** 493
- **Fat:** 49g
- **Protein:** 5g
- **Carbs:** 8g

## 49. Chocolate Peanut Butter Shake

**Preparation time:** 5 minutes.

**Cooking time:** 0 minutes.

**Servings:** 2

**Ingredients:**
- 2 bananas
- 3 tablespoons peanut butter
- 1 cup almond milk
- 3 tablespoons cacao powder

**Directions:**
1. Combine all the ingredients in a blender until smooth.

**Nutrition:**
- **Calories:** 149
- **Fat:** 1.1g
- **Carbohydrates:** 1.5g
- **Protein:** 7.9g

## 50. Chia Coffee Mix

**Preparation time:** 15 minutes.

**Cooking time:** 0 minutes.

**Servings:** 1

**Ingredients:**
- 1 tablespoon chia seeds
- 2 cups strongly brewed coffee, chilled
- 1 ounce macadamia nuts
- 1–2 packets stevia, optional
- 1 tablespoon MCT oil

**Directions:**
1. Add all the listed ingredients to a blender. Blend on high until smooth and creamy. Enjoy your smoothie!

**Nutrition:**
- **Calories:** 395
- **Fat:** 39g
- **Carbohydrates:** 11g
- **Protein:** 5.2g

## 51. Lime and Cucumber Electrolyte Drink

**Preparation time:** 5 minutes.

**Cooking time:** 0 minutes.

**Servings:** 4

**Ingredients:**
- ¼ cup chopped cucumber
- 1 tablespoon fresh lime juice
- 1 tablespoon apple cider vinegar
- 2 tablespoons maple syrup
- ¼ teaspoon sea salt, optional
- 4 cups water

**Directions:**
1. Combine all the ingredients in a glass. Stir to mix well.
2. Refrigerate overnight before serving.

**Nutrition:**
- **Calories:** 114
- **Fat:** 0.1g
- **Carbs:** 28.9g
- **Fiber:** 0.3g
- **Protein:** 0.3g

## 52. Plant-Based Strawberry Cream

**Preparation time:** 5 minutes.

**Cooking time:** 0 minutes.

**Servings:** 2

**Ingredients:**
- 1 cup of frozen strawberries
- 1/3 cup raw cashew butter
- 1/3 cup non-dairy plain yogurt
- 2 teaspoons fresh lemon juice
- 1/8 teaspoon salt

**Directions:**
1. Add all the ingredients to a food processor and process until it gets wet and chunky.
2. Scrape the sides and bottom well and process again for a couple of minutes until completely smooth and well mixed.
3. Pour mixture in container and chill for a couple of hours or overnight. Spread it over whole-grain bread. Enjoy!

**Nutrition:**
- **Calories:** 141
- **Carbs:** 14g
- **Fat:** 8g
- **Protein:** 2g

## 53. Tropi-Kale Breeze

**Preparation time:** 5 minutes.

**Cooking time:** 0 minutes.

**Servings:** 3-4

**Ingredients:**
- 1 cup chopped pineapple (frozen or fresh)
- 1 cup chopped mango (frozen or fresh)
- ½ to 1 cup chopped kale
- ½ avocado
- ½ cup of coconut milk
- 1 cup water or coconut water
- 1 teaspoon matcha green tea powder (optional)

**Directions:**
1. Purée everything in a blender until smooth, adding more water (or coconut milk) if needed.

**Nutrition:**
- **Calories:** 566
- **Fat:** 36g
- **Carbs:** 66g
- **Protein:** 8g

# Conclusion

Thank you for making it to the end of this book. I hope you found lots of tasty recipes that satisfied you.
If you want to know all the benefits of the vegetarian diet, applied not only to smoothies and juices, but also to other foods and meals, from the same series you can find:

**PLANT BASED DIET: THE BENEFITS**

**PLANT BASED DIET COOKBOOK: RECIPES FOR YOUR BREAKFAST**

**PLANT BASED DIET COOKBOOK: RECIPES FOR YOUR LUNCH**

**PLANT BASED DIET COOKBOOK: RECIPES FOR YOUR DINNER**

**PLANT BASED DIET COOKBOOK: RECIPES FOR YOUR SALADS**

**PLANT BASED DIET COOKBOOK: RECIPES FOR YOUR DESSERTS**

# PLANT BASED DIET COOKBOOK: SUPERFOODS RECIPES

# PLANT BASED DIET COOKBOOK: ALKALINE FOODS RECIPES

www.ingramcontent.com/pod-product-compliance
Lightning Source LLC
Chambersburg PA
CBHW060043230426
43661CB00004B/640